Abstract Rulz

By

David Calderhead

This book is a work of non-fiction. Names and places have been changed to protect the privacy of all individuals. The events and situations are true..

ISBN: 1-4140-3664-7 (e-book)
ISBN: 1-4140-3663-9 (Paperback)

Library of Congress Control Number: 203098494

This book is printed on acid free paper.

Printed in the United States of America
Bloomington, IN

1stBooks - rev. 12/30/03

CHAPTER 1

Solidified Natures

Decisions, an inner collision between two opposing natures. Knowing this, I am forced down the hallway of discontent. I am generally speaking with no generality...spitting in jest, wind blown, skyward in Northern Straights.

I feel in multiple conjectures. They are imposing. They impose their tiny inhibitions on my imprint. They are fools in traps self-imposed. lines of barracudas up through the nose, dimples and whistles. They are silly surreal characters...just another day trying not to make any sense, non-sense pouring out of the disjointed membrane.

Animals and bugs un-named, unknown, unimagined. Animals and bugs unseen, unsown...living a life in seclusion, I am. Disillusion and confusion, I am. I went off to the hot springs, went down into the heat. I went into the steam to moan...alone...I did not want to be disturbed. I did not want to be disturbed by any life that I never lived, would never live. I did not disturb the hot, heady waters.

Cognition...a reoccurrence reoccurring. echoes... echoes... echoes... every faster through the tilting, close to tumbling hallways of my discontent. Constant inebriation is a short reality away...and thank you. Thank you, but remember: there is no next time in this convoluted nature. There is no next time...

Reality is the disease of sobriety. Everything has this soil at its base. This soil grows new flowers after depletion, utter depletion.

These flowers are strange. Sick of the cure...sick of the cure...sick of the cure. More poison is needed. More poison is sought....

Solidified natures...crystallizing occurrences. I watch the dog growl after invisible doorways open and close.... The current flows northeast, dragged down the beach in front of hot whores and great expectations. Splendid fact-counting insurance keeps the hipsters at bay...for a while at least.

I looked up into the windows of the 14th floor. I saw myself staring back at me. Who fucking cares? Who has the strength to go through the motions anymore anyway....winds blowing. I can barely think. I live the day each day as it approaches, as it engulfs me, as it abandons me...blue hues and God's mental mastery.

I am starting to get comfortable in my shell though my spirit still cries for remembrance...where is my spirit anyway? Where does His mansion sit? Does He wait eagerly for past payments? Cheating disillusions mask my soul's secret hallways—perfect peace has its say and doggedness...redundant drudgery...is whisked away...away...Who has the answer? Who's got the damn map?

It's so sad to be completely lost with no home to manifest that which is considered psychologically sound—no meds, if you please. Wouldn't it be nice to fit in your mind psychologically? But then, what is the mind? Is the mind the brain? Switch before it's too late…let's switch all the rules around when it comes to creative stroking of the imagination.

CHAPTER 2

Sin So Seductive…

Stones…brick roads heaving…breathing…rolling down alleyways, leading to hell or even eternity's door. If there is life, I can't see it.

Words carry sweet intoxication and empathy. They boil slowly. I hold my breath. I keep my mouth closed…tight.

You…I saw you, and I tripped a bit in the rhetorical realm…If I could just find the right words…I tripped and the words fell out of me…scurried away like insects to hide under the rocks, in the walls, behind the door…I looked up at you…wordlessly…

Kings and queens…I am sickened by their reality…by their choke hold on it. But they own the bridge over it…exact a toll to cross…I feel my heart miss a beat…the kings and queens grin wickedly…I am free to walk over to the other side. I cross…

You again…I imagine you…I almost stumble and fall…I can't look back or digress. But your beauty blurs my vision. I put you out of mind. My vision clears. I get to my feet…I make my way again…Am I walking in place…perpetual futility…an insane tune repeating itself endlessly in my head…

Specters…dark obsessions…within me…whip about…moths hungry for flame…demean me. I would board sanity's train as I would cross the bridge. I would gladly let the train carry me, rocking gently, to reality. I look out at fields as the trains passes. I see scarecrows staked out…abandoned versions of myself. The young are playing games in the fields at the feet of the scarecrows…In the window, faintly, I see an old man staring back at me…heavy eyes….

There is no objective point to going on…to pursue…slow carnage within…atrocities…I go. I pursue. Then, there you are…unbidden…a presence…I trip on your scene…selective, intact, jointed with death…spewing forth the atrocities into some unnamed, uncharted cataclysm, a maze: hands reach up toward a heaven long razed. I avert my eyes from the window. I close them…to keep the nightmare in.

Come out…my spirit comes out while I am walking the black fields containing hollow gravestones. I touch each one in passing, hoping to hear an echo of myself. I am looking for me here. I am sure I am here. I leave an imprint, an impression of myself on everything. I watch as some gravestones crumble and grave flowers wilt. All that unhappy flesh held down, muffled by the earth…temporal…brains working well to recognize that breathing and afflictions dance together, first one and then the other leading…to this place. Hot winds swirls…strange…I am disoriented first…nauseous…then I am at peace…I am serene. I have arisen from these dead, from their dirty, cold sleep. Tiny demons attack me…bounce off me…disappear. I have shed them like bacteria…sightless wandering…cool day to caste forth some castrating directive.

Spirit…in spirit, blood holds…holds lofty gifts of valor…I was sitting on the horse at the back of the stage show…the horse and I were talking…reminiscing…laughing…we reminded each other of each other…ha-ha-ha…A ritual holds off the onslaught of demons for a very short time…long and fluid transgressions…holding onto misty, wet air…wanting to fall in love with a vision…still unattached…I traveled for a while on red roads…into the cool wading water…below the pasqual moon…the sky's lofty glare…I came to a sport on the path that leads straight…following a jagged path…to lover's square…lovers dance without a care…death does not consume illusion…is an illusion…knives and spoons thrown up into the air…falling…clanking off black tiled floors…the horse and I stare at one another…wonder what it all means.

Who knows…who knows the get up or ties…consciousness shines down on humanity's tepid insecurities. I looked with sort of a sideways glance at that which rolls off my back for creativity…found innumerable amounts of soul-searching imagination…it was as if I had found gates which lead to eternal bastardly ruin…I promptly turned away…with a flash of my hand…with a flash of my hand I bid farewell once and for all to thoughts of rhetorical damnation…so worldly…so unsurreal…what's the matter with the abstract core of delusion…skip the grind…no more dead ends masquerading as new beginnings…wicked control…master reality fucking flock…faster and faster.

Decisive...decisive and congenial in an annihilated fashion...we sulked in slumber before light flashed out of our being...willful anarchy...imaginative configurations. I went down to the lake today and serenity enveloped my stature in thick rainbow colors...fluorescent...gray...solid block institutions at the core of every delighted destiny...poetic outburst...liquid lyrics create a new pathway to the unknown...rhetorical sense leads to concrete, dense and weighted down...still the spirit seeps through...it sure beats time...chokehold over humanity...doesn't it. I have to find a clear pasture in my mind...a place to graze...a place to wander alone...obsessions and compulsions and rituals repulsive...out to pasture...snakes in the grass...not gonna give it to you this time...senseless beyond the stone gate...our mental state.

It was an eve drooping over the sightless which reacted so vulgarly to eager insinuations. Black light shines its forms over meandering communication...pre-warned bullet collage and amnesty intact.

It's now more than ever a zoom lens for bones intact. Zealous mountains overlook innumerable ants on their pathways and in their holes...alive one against the backdrop of rotting skins. It all makes its way into the secretive drip amidst a tantalizing effect. Why is the dream always so much better than the reality? Breathing your last breaths on depression's concrete bridge...what does it mean anyway? The unalterable fate awaits us all. Why does apathy shoot its razor-edge arrows at the flock? Though your addictions may bind you, your fears will never find you...and telepathy will be the path that leads your way. Walls full of spears, soaked with blood in bodies full of moronic courage. Bees and flies in the outer room while the corpse awaits its fate. Letter full of apologetic chatter, thinking you had practitioners by the balls...peeking through the cracks from the clear down below...dirty men living on the flipside of mourning...an open field brigade, loose and comatose under the pavement...a vertical blue bent on virtual upheaval. Learn your lessons in society's holes...boxes full of mind control...tasting salty water in the roof of someone else's mouth...looking through another's stoned eyes...seeing yet another pasqual disguise.

In a million alternative realities lies millions of blazing eternities, I didn't make the days nor invent the nights of stellar decree...stoic mystery spewing out of the stranger's box...which I'll never see. Sometimes it seems I'll never get through, so I keep on trudging along underneath the blue moon and the electric sun...searching for that high in the sky.

Let's trade and labor and find our way into the elastic ecstatic and numb identity. I was high in the mountains looking out across forever...my mind erased and reduced itself to its own initial subconscious refrain. I see God coming down the trail...or is that the devil's crew trying to spread their wings over my town? Superficiality squeezes down its claws on passive flesh. Massive innuendo, sporadic hyper veins make roads into utopia's stupor. A nauseated freedom makes for white shadows behind the cult's sanctuary...whirling around like and injured bug on its way to slow death and debauchery…dying to meet your inner fall…to heed your deafening call…sadistic outpouring of a cosmic emotion as yet unidentified.

Sick of reality masters and their god-like statures…much like a society slave or a rhetoric-stuck monk…there's nothing that resembles a revolution of thought which is desperately needed…crumbling mass intuition and body-trance…illusion moving on to the grim award of merit…side slip perception which carries a bundle in the afterworld…a crafty line of salvation and the inner brain of starvation…testing the outer boundaries with no solid ground to walk upon.

Now the nature we inhale will one day become stale and hanging, and hanging onto the breeze will one day become unattainable…no base or starting point to contend with…a spectator at a barroom brawls and liquor-brewed agitation…spilled guts…spilled guts and special days of reunion combine to form the greatest of all bastards of heavenly lineage. It's all a passive indifference flying around in the around…alienated by mental heretics masquerading as disorders…not relaxed without a substance of some sort or the other. Low flying demons spread perplexity as an inherited lot…sleepy-eyed reunions with a perfumed corpse annihilate in the flood gates in the upper chamber.

Body-wrapped coil-like in a snow-white death…an aforementioned thought process has its idiosyncrasies which are used as a shield to fight unseen demons. We, being of radical descent, award ourselves in the outer region with continual, stoned delays as a gift…suicide-live electric and a rigid cast-iron directive. So as we go on, the first one holds down the weight, and the second one's absurd. To erase a bad picture is permissible when needed and the six is forbidden. Sweaty, wet music with a spastic walking: the mist begins talking in jibberish or a foreign language, I'm not sure which…No strong suite to play or hidden forays, nothing but lost…well shaken deities…spherical entities in the cool aberrations decisiveness. Displays of rigidity bounce off walls of silence into the realm of resurgence. Depression is a two-edged blade, and there's blood soaking in the stranger's eyes.

A radical, incessant diatribe, just inches away from creativity…a purple bludgeoning fear…God sent and ripped through the extremities. A motionless conscience stole its breath from an outer, hyper disposition. No definition is accurate, yet a few words in the swarm like surreal, liquid, poetical, disjointed free forms. Spill your guts on the river you're standing upon. Associations with moody spirits create a two-sided barrage of intricate design…always on the stairway edge of the mountain side of a picturesque beauty. Sin is so seductive, and so is all that causes momentary bliss…seaweed on the bottom and amazing spectrals in the evening sky. So fucking what? It's just another seesaw night spent with diseased thought. Radical influx in fields of heat. Count yourself one of the lucky ones in the grand parade…stealth agitation in the foaming sea…salt in the roof of my mouth and in the back of my thought…ancient reactions to go up to the moment...grim prospects. All that it is is reproachable bodies of death and spoon-fed elders who went a little too far. As the spiral winds down, so the evil rises. Repercussions hiding behind rotted wood blinds. The abstract has its rules, you know...must be obeyed. How about a carnal reject to fathom irresponsibly...coastal lines in the forefront of a deadly degradation...free-form agitation in the inside shell makes it hard to breathe a simple breath of thick cold air. Death from fair intoxication and slow mystical reproach...proving grounds in the foxtail of night and magic reverberations...everything reverberates in sound's lusty cauldrom...no more monotony or fancy dress...go off on your trails alone.

CHAPTER 3

Crazy Blue

Not normal streams of straight thinking being crushed beneath sanity's floor. Insane rules keep the lepers at bay for a while. Respect for those who took the plunge into the rainbow sea. No good dejection as a spiritual clue. Through the abstract, we come to that which is a surreal notion. The light slowly fades to darkness where you are walking. Your candle fades, and as if in black ink, you are surrounded. But, if you walk far enough, you'll eventually be covered in shiny golden light...awesome discovery: a disjointed rabid inflection of camaraderie on the enemy's behalf; predisposed inner eagles flying in all directions; clichéd metallic henchman struck with disease of despondency.

No rules here. No customs to distract creators. No rituals. No reality-based hedonists who refuse to take the blame for the heat wave of rhetoric, red hot, wandering the moist cemetery. There are so many variables in the quick-spreading, all encompassing dilemma.

There are spots on the blood-stained cathedral walls. I want nothing; I want it all. I have been forgiven before...it's a bad taste in my mouth. What am I...drugged up fanatic free for all to act out, free to be absurd, free to distract all those commanders of boredom. Nothing up my sleeves. Watch me flip.

Innumerable crass conflicts in the masses, the source of all that is funny, all that is me, my creative substance in time. Thought you were lost, but you never walked that far, where the lighted city let of its friendly glow, the look of safety, a good night's sleep. So now it's time to go, and what did this high-spirited babble mean? Throw the man a bone and lead him into the fields of sunshine. Whitish degrees of unfinished blues shatter the air. Nestled high above the gleaming clear water is a philosophy of man's inner vein... throbbing. The moon shines down on human interests as though on a dust cloud...glowing, but forlorn. Sincere albeit fascinating castration haunted webs exuberant and full of angry suspicions, expanding in the atmosphere of the abstract...

It's not time for any coaxing on the part of the old medieval saints...only...only poetic blasts of incorrigible, throw-away dysfunction...no panic in the trees, only misjudged comedy...nobody gets it...no clout, no conclusion. Standard serenity...bottled in foreign land by long-forgotten rules...monotony's last stand...well, leaning against a wall. Take out the whip and stay a while.

Undue dispensing of non-thought out, non-rational procedures...vast complexities...infernal...my attention span melts. Ragged symphonic previews...music before the music...dreary in their constant fury. Adversaries brushed aside like dust on a coffee table. Exact precisions mad and gleeful and stocked...sober fury. Approachable only by means of attrition...staunch...rehabilitative fraud. Passion soaked dismemberment in the sky. Learn the startled stare and shake the striptease flattery…indigestion. A mere moment…confined question…about the cemetery lot…those with skin…new insinuations about…heat.

The psychotic road leads straight into Heaven's openings. The imagined air thickening but undermined…feels like an over-crowded ocean.…unreachable stars in impenetrable night…beautiful. The assassinations of free minds lead to the instant gratification of the ultimate foreman who is ever asleep on the job. How can you kill death when you're supposed to live life…lazy innuendos have no place in the inner sanitarium.

The stark naked stay that way…the sky has no explanation for the endless aerial maneuvers that aggravate…in the sky with sighs…too much flow and blasted bits of years gone by…rows of skeletal remains dancing in ecstasy hanging from hooks in the examination room…bones flying in all directions…eyes unseen. Proud issuance of golden stones to the overly dense populations…can't be baked, can't be burned.

Tripping balls into mental halls, finding pleasure where pain is…always in the vein…so glad to be here…now let me go…sold…ruins in rooms of ruined rooms…to get upstairs you must go downstairs past the sleeping foreman who will see you…smell the rotting odor of death…splattered remnants on super trips leading the monotonous mule…assume the position of slaves to unknown gods…senseless and senile…

All a facsimile…a faux metaphor…a false figure…you're falling through it…unexpressed dialogue locked in a trance…undone interest in a cold conclave of diamond-hard awe. It's tough to express heartless seconds of weariness with incorrigible, rust-resistant words. Heartless affection sees the inner the inner void as some comic rock…touch and tells you a new joke…laugh and laugh…a sea of trepidation and disappointment…ruthless awesome glee. The arrival of infliction with a cheery mood…ponder that. Unappraochable dogs…growling, lubricated by drool…hackles raised…I just want to touch the blue sky…

Forward to enchantment with faceless hipsters undressing…rhetoric, screw off; common sense be damned. Liars from a cult which no one in his right mind ever joins watches the hipsters, the exposed flesh enviously…no lie. Fascination is disillusion and death. Eloquence beyond the dome of the castrated sky. Pride and mysteries make for an uncondoned rise in missed amnesia. Insincere group gratification sessions infest apologetic reactions in infernal spaces.

Singing songs on a morphine dream…pitch black lights meandering in devilish gray. Off comes the robe of mercy only to be replaced in a robe of swarming angels. Presently speaking to the sparks which surround the overcrowded pathway called earth. Round and round the mental view where clues consisting of frozen matter can be found and inspected. Frosty prose started out as a firmament of biblical proportions and lost wages from yesterday's spendthrift. Control the battered click and catapult the mules to higher learning.

Suspect the countless accounts of benevolence on the outer rim of consciousness. Superior and clear images come through timed and masked forever...Cotton mouth parades while lakes of sun beat down with jackhammer precision. Cold beverage stands and icy moods shake the brick foundations. No retape in the concrete will fulfill sedation of a few inner relations with the checkerboard drudgery of home. It's just what it takes for temporary purple alienation. That sorrow filled sun can't wait another day to be bastardized along with the reset of the skiddish lot. Let's make this carnal acceptance speech a thorn in the ancient side. Forget the past and its moodiness, pleasant and otherwise...force the axe into space. Do your chores at the dilapidated monastery of youth and its maggot-infested sister.

Complete anti-sensual delay in the boiling muck of intensity. Immense time...superficial time beckons for solitude...dull but delightful in the illusionary tact of the phase I am going through...Never adjust the attitude (not the altitude) to correspond with a spiritual forest and the creatures lurking therein...

Assume the disappearance of other worldly activity. Live the pure life in the concrete jungle...No time for colors or shifting hues...no time for anything generalized or assumed...

The countless graces of the as-yet, great unfinished lyric...the singer incomplete and as-yet unconscious, too.

17

Why does rage seep through my eyelids and out into the world to threaten all peace and serenity…the solitude of my shining sun? Open spaces and gunfire. The explosions at first burst forth as if I am creating my own tiny novas in all directions. The darkness does not die.

Plagiarized, synthesized, and sanitized: my mind, and so I set forth to paint the sky with skills learned from Dali. A quick, unkept dawn has it style down to the last dot. An absentee frolic in the sessions where the binary is of two minds…each thought thus the square of the previous thought…and me with no aspirins…only aspirations.

Mother Nature died. Do not send any condolences from this sack of packed flesh. There can be no flowers, of course. There are no flowers.

So who's the addicted one now? It isn't me anymore. Programmed solititude…solidified natures are petty situations meant to see the real sunlight…

Stacked books in the rafters. It's all going to be all right. It's going to be as free as a deadening ritual in the heart, its own lovely deception. Ivy vines and trees down below have been accosted by soft, false participants in the moaning nightfall. Blood trees full of grotesque scabs and indifference…there you will find me…good hunting…

Breathing.

CHAPTER 4

Lovers' Dances

Free…for-all dreams…I escaped from the tight trip…finally. Crass-intentioned ambition in the sweat shop on the moon. In the slow-motion moment, everything has such subtle movements…great movements of raw pails of death. Moving bodies singing along to a joyous song of degradation…decadence give rise to heredity and bones joined at the joint…a backward system held accountable by a crashing view of a drained swamp…all those things…all those things there writhing in the mud, the muck, the fetid muck…hold back the sighting of a deepened, main view in the blood thirsty monstrosity of perpetual motion…keep doing that…keep doing that…yes, that…

Sin…your sin…judged…judged and found wanting…mediocre…mediocre and obsessed…obsessed and full of twisted cuts and bruises…what are you doing?…kiss the whitewater…lick the breeze…find your way into the forbidden hall…anybody got a light?…associations in conflict in the deafening courtyard…sound out superficially and monotonous…

A clear creative work is rare and scarce on the roadways and in the palaces…a solitary voice singing along the empty highways…in the empty rooms…the air stirs…becomes a little wind…listens…whirls about in a little dance…falls back into itself...falls asleep again...dreams...forgets...who are you?...where did you go?

Long gone...long gone days...and degrees of a friendly expression...faces made in the mirror...the foggy mirror...tattoo with lipstick kisses...I'm looking for you...rats hit the wall at a frenzied pace...just like dogs in the sky...I'm looking for you...I see the spiders' eyes and feel the glorification and the justification...I'm looking for you...I am traveling through the dizzy head on sold waterways at mind-boggling speeds...so goes the artistic loser a blind spot as a back view...

Half conscious from the wonder drug which stagnates hip suggestion...is that you over there? Trees swim with a hip swagger and breath toxic cherry air...oh, how I want you again...oh, how I want...river spot encourages lead spastic illuminations to the ultimate flame...I burn...burn with me...

Campaigns...you again...raggedy and differing campaigns of trust undeniable...not like an evil aspiration...you again...inject the venom and deny the earth's sole tragedy. Haphazard, introspective seeds grown in the spirit-filled fields...medical aspects unconcerned with this history, the charade...I'm so glad you came back...green muting...a fire wall...the two assume wretched countenance as a control mechanism...

Suspect stormy conditions on your way to free associations...take me with you...I want to go...suspense-ridden riddle of flame and point three messengers...they were the same all the time…sheep…white whales bathe in the rainbow of perception…solo island parade with pompous island women in love with their own disturbed bag of smack…a hospital's maddening delight with spoonfuls of reactions…innumerable space heirs and melancholy…I'm free…perfectly inept, yet still functionally opposed to any paper reward…I'm free…

Mass…it's just like mass acceptance of international fraud and a tinge, a tiny tinge of fascism…enough to make you sit up and take notice…heil, heil, heil…real, true designated degrees of sainthood, going up and up through the air of incompetence and deleted thought of yesterday's shadow assume importance among the flock.

Comical…a comical frown scares the legions of practicing angels. It's high time for the dust to clear and another stoned trip to purgatory. Annihilate constant, vertical correction an enter the chamber of lost souls. Rarely is anything considered except for burnt youth…and struggling age.

Sunlight…as the sunlight seemingly melts this city into light and liquid, I begin…I begin listening for my calling. Across barren lands, I run, opposed to any false conceptions. There's no leader who's denied acceptance into the brotherhood of the abstract opposing rhymes, opposing seasons…no lukewarm cast-out eternity.

Cold…it's so cold here…just hanging onto the breeze. Accusatory hyperactivity making known reactions to recognition…

Perfectly loose and prophetic…a retrospective recluse unable to find an outlet for the yearnings from the gut. The spectacle approaching became unabashed, potent illusion…clamoring for anything but mystic, red showers…pretty hip chicks walking with arrogant swagger…approaching obscenities at all points…and here and there a little tinge of serenity.

Evil…there's no evil or good in the overly sedated courtyards of peace…70 miles an hour into the backwoods where lies are kept secret and stagnate…separated, absentminded language understood by all mankind…left out in the yard to meander foolishly around like cattle. Much of the year has passed and yet my brain still lingers in consciousness. Special mentally speaking must stretch out the thought process irreversibly.

Complete the catastrophes that await this earth and do it in quick manner so those that are left can get on with things…an abstract attack along the lines of a continuous feud found only in tranquility…an integral part of crisp, cool air, feeling substance in the rain and king-like in the sun.

A massive thrift store like reality sale await monetary consumption from the labor pool: scarce, rigid, repulsive competition in the lower ranks…leave out the internal repetition of days left unspoken for where you once heard the lions roar and also never drown. There is a lull in creativity's state these days…a new direction and destination desperately needed stoked for the outer atmosphere in delayed hipster moves. Daily the grind gets soaking wet from overuse.

Creative errors in the hip scene of old, worn out retribution…accumulated, so-called cool soldiers lost in society's web…arriving at the last possible point in time…imaginable. Perhaps cold showers in the summer heat will satisfy inner longings for that which was lost…worn out aspirations shiver and move in worm-like shapes. Pump the mules out like stolen gods. Fill their minds with repetition and flirtatious glances…memory approaching evil loads of a more catastrophic nature. Will bombs wake up the deranged or will they fall asleep faster? It's been said that you can't start without the origin of a will…that nonsense is why creativity's in the poor state that it's in right now…a poetic interrogation where the rhetorical poet is cast once and for all. There are a million reasons to blaze. Flirtatious glances from the heathen hold down below where the outcasts go and gather in unison…bent on sore means of courage and retractable slits of light that lead to the passive and has cause for benevolence.

Sick and uneventful… the snake that bit nature's heels was boredom. The higher calling actually comes in a piercing silence that comes to the subject involved over and over again…take care of mental hygiene with a daily mind flush that allows for smooth, free-flowing thought…millions for lives that will never be found underground or below the bottom of the sea…exist without human eyes to see. Times spent as a chameleon in a rainbow blaze cursed by the moon will one day cause relations between spiritual fakes to cease any further activity.

Never...never use constant repercussions as by-laws for inner destinations. The messy little man with the eager smile stood in the middle to the third level and laughed himself to tears...reactionary visionary uphill approach to senility...perpetual madness rests in the hearts with the spirit as an anchor living in a spider web, crawling around with ant heads in a surreal stream of consciousness...separating the coarse, stubborn brain extracting all rhetorical secretions...hot attractions in the midnight sun...go and be energized and be on your way. Freezing in the sunshine...and lying when the truth is spotless and clear.

CHAPTER 5

Slaves in Armor

Fancy dress décor among fools...roles and ugly untolds...wondering how the day breaks out of its mold, among symbolic lock and key, among flesh and gold. The cardinal sin is not so prophetic, but is unabashed and unafraid with perfect clarity and intuition. Years roll swiftly by an armed trance in spiritual moods...sail out of the ocean of rhetorical consumption. Depletion of outer and golden triangles and all that's left is complementary sin...imperfection all around...sick of pretty people and their own perfect sound...filling up spaces with aspirations and misdeeds...sounds from the insincere brain trust that's been left behind...happy center moods with a dog's view...they forever attach themselves...any other way to get back from the trek into awakening...in depth and slow decay...there's not enough aura left in the quota man...dirty dungeons in the heart of the desperate city waiting on dust-free oak to capture all essentialities. After the frequent visions of moods without congeniality, we're left with no alternative except for a radical fluctuation...out when it gets beyond local...fanatical in what you get to hear in normal protection is what gods have...and that is all that matters...approximating in the depth of superficiality, there's a hairline fracture indulged in finding its fate. Night time retrospective breeds only thin relief by the higher deities…not accepting the fact that there's only one…greasy reaction to an outer mental stupor…find the ghost in the backyard…drag him by the neck and kick him through the front…rain-stained glass remains in the fight in a forward that has already been…already been written…fresh in the imagination dwelt with loosely under the bottom of the ocean…freaks float forward…in my mental nature. Your flippant attitude makes furry shells rampant in the overview. He who is born in the minute depletion of ineptitude is bound to attract scattered nuances like fleas. ..specialty clues die in the back view…access demeaning allure into fine points of brackish light…learning sooner or later the ground has many names…which spur humanity onward…congratulate thorns as they decide to win their present struggle…in a candid crush of a long forgotten charade…a satire is traded for apathy.

CHAPTER 6

Three Stone Fabric

Tulip marchers, one by one, soaked and saturated themselves before given a chance to live. As a con artist leads his crew into a passive danger, so the red flock is walking freely into paths unknown. There's common knowledge that all fools were kings in another life aside from reincarnation. Confused sparkles and spirits of lost gold mines betrayed, held in constant obtrusiveness: shoes with no cover can sure consume debauchery. Incident-prone dialects take sugary steaks to the town: never seen such a waste of decent pawns walking onward into garbage. The effect of the long-haired, wishy-washy demon is over. Stupendous occasions are horrific...oh, they're grand. Mess up the moon's interpretation with a basic grin. Move your eyes upward and up into death. New wines bring talking stones to the post. Seeing the subconscious as a separate entity is like being in the stomach of the lion. Enroll in the school of thought and come out a rhetorically stuck monk: didn't know who I was until I reached her final cunt...place of rest. A man that lives under the ocean bottom finally found a place to rest. Windows and cars eat a melodramatic cause. In the nature of things, all fripple back to incessant diatribes.

Stunning inhibitions are distasteful. Back blood flows into blood-soaked crevices in the cave. It may be sensible to avoid that which entangles all slip trip-loaded logic. Loaded pistol grips with live invocations play the snotty hand, take it through the seductive loop. Whores spin in seductive circles totally oblivious to outer cries. The morning descends with a quickness upon stolen logic...soaked lightly in a dream's death, ending in arrow straights on an icy cruise. Someone is holding someone's mediocrity up in the air...night time atrocities on some planet in a mercury bowl...armies of rarities, stoned pathological eye. Scared paranoid strong arms leave the house in hasty motions. Pity lost its strangle hold in long, backward strikes. When the calling card comes back into social, sacred prominence, then we'll know...we'll know starry-eyed peace. Hate the lion, sour mane and reactive...all that doesn't insist on drudgery. Inept at clinical reclusiveness where power is considered useful, catastrophe grips the inner eye with an iron grip...no way out.

CHAPTER 7

Waves of Euphoria

A small interrogation in the repetitive abundance of solo adjectives...babbling inanities scattered love...bullshit. Liquid lust and paranoid distrust to the golden city of the immaculate craziness...mental rides to the spiritually mundane event...souls and gold dripping from the magnetic sky...looters rising...no one knows where he will go and distracts anymore...justified distractions...speak in slow breathing movements...don't be afraid...change a high held view...recreators and instigators mesmerize uncanny directives...loose cannons in hell wonder at the crease...used to listen to a man I once knew...used to...on his head was a diamond-bright blue.

The peace on the globe is ready for disaster. The amusement of the brethren enlist enlightenment as an objective...sensitivity to the crooked freedomized by millions of holes in the glass. Down in the depth in the section east of martyrdom is a viable defection in detection...grab a handful...surprising weight...spin it around the false gods full of ridiculous smiles. Track-free human dogs run rampant in the winter streets, as they often do, never retreat from an honest form. A literal, insecure madness obtains navy-blue insects to flow in a perfect militant attitude...freefall with noble flames at the base for assurance. Predominance holds sway, sick of the pretty-people brigade…a vindictive secretion full of snotty holes in the atmosphere. Speculative breeding grounds don't need an adult-spewed seclusions…sublimation in the hearts of many…a crazy catechism: the only air in the grave…prolific endeavors in the cool rain…upside down to reproduce…get it right. Grey is a blazing fire and therefore cannot be used to suffocate.

Build flat mountains which shine in the sunshine and blow away the wind. Down, way down in a full, bottomless, empty ditch may some unknown new society exist. Continuous impartiality parades itself like some bastardly bitch. Rituals die hard. Mask scrutiny shows no mercy or empathy with the witch doctor. A hedonistic, self-contained dope fiend refused because of a locked up brain stain…appeasement for the crypt in general usage personified. Purple present jaunts into the forest where death originated . Conditions of a paradise race extravagantly and smoothly, ending in nobility. Experience destitution…substitute for rage and empathy, a constitute of dogma. Keep reactionary visions in a padded, locked box, never allowing them to scurry away. Please ask the doorman to exceed all predecessors in mundane monotony…filled to the top with cast-iron rigidity…all but changed…all but seated in a resumed-like bag of singular spots and checks…maybe skiddish like bone soaked in blood…delightful for a moment…desired for a few more. Purpose that is never…long-shaded purposes of perception.

Obscure reflection on the memory trip. Don't succeed the commander's ode to philosophical anarchy. Do your best to far-out outwit inner and further bullshit. The mushrooms await their days in canisters…fields of spite in valleys and in streams of poisons, death's brew. Too much order leads to anarchy and chaos. Anarchy and chaos lead to a semblance of a new order. Profound seclusion from the big orgy in the sky. Renowned invocation in the backyard fence…don't believe that obscenity will cover up willing interpretation of indignation…shifty black skin shining and glistening in the midday gloom. There are discrepancies in blue and red…contact with unworldly eyes. The funeral procession marches through the street delayed in the smoldering wind personal inner clarity…outer, insidious, insinuating delicacy. A subtle double crossing of the highest yield…procedure ousted from the sickbed of earth by a tyrannical tide of mourning. Hula loops in the window seal—thriving off scarcely clad repugnant chips of waste.

32

CHAPTER 8

Beyond the Wrath of Contemplation

Beyond everything...clearly seen...and all that is stumbled upon...beyond human understanding and the all-important self...it's there before us...but it's not. It...the Big It...begins with dementia, and it begins with clarity, too. It has no end and no beginning...we created reason to battle it. To define it we worship whatever we made it appear to be, yet it's incomprehensible and elusive. It makes us ask questions, yet it gives us no answers...or maybe it does: we just don't know how to listen. Since we can't see it, we dismiss it, yet it's always there guiding and calling in mysterious ways.

This I that I am...I know is a complete sham, so I struggle to fight free to find this force that eludes me...this force I cannot grasp is beyond the wrath of contemplation. Consistent mental traffic...can't stop thinking that I wish I could stop thinking...just for one moment, one moment of total amnesia...a one-time blackout coming back with faculties intact...a sleeping rage, full on, head blown. Paranoid bits and pieces of me...drifting out...flying away...so I can finally see...so I can sleep another day.

The world and its weird itinerary always remains to me a mystery...a strange inconsistency. Everything I think is the truth turns out to be a lie. Every time I feel a yearning to live, my time clock tells me soon I'll die. I cannot face this craziness. I can't keep up in the image race. So, I breed and carry on. I sing the same old song of monetary freedom. I'm just a chameleon running in the wind. I've been so very far, but I'm not sure where I've been. I've been so many places that it's sometimes hard to tell. I've never seen Heaven, but I feel I've been to hell.

Watching candle wax drip down the wall…sitting idly back…focusing on nothing at all…What should I do? I think I'll let God make the call to me…pampered, prison soul on top of the world…I know…a rhetoric-stuck monk finally breaking free…a deafening comparison…mind set in still thinking…stirring up souls beneath the cave…another dog day done.

Life came to me, and I left it over there…even though all I had left was an inner feeling of despair. I was lost in another's blood…held up by the sun. So, I keep on trudging along into the blue light…into the electric night…beyond the rhetorical stare and the moon's lofty glare. Death came to me. I left it over there even though the life I lived never seemed very clear…grounded beneath the spacious space, never wanting to see another face. Keep tripping your balls off…into the sky's allure…into God's human cure…beyond the pathological eye…beyond the endless cry.

I feel like I'm crushed underneath a frozen soul in retreat. My spirit is mesmerized. My numb head is hypnotized, and there I'll lie and there I'll die…crushed underneath. War within beneath the skin…a battle inside where the spirits collide. Gone are the times we worried and prayed and left our demons to die with the day. Gone are the years we laid in the sun, forgot our differences, dropped our guns. Gone are the moments when peace paralyzed our souls...writings in time of religious inspiration...man thought not...turned is back and lost his eternal invitation...killed his God for bodily suffocation...will kill himself with spiritual deprivation.

I see dispassionate continuities of grandeur. I see hypocrites wearing fancy dress...a loss of blood and slow showers with drops falling on dead skin. I see haunting faces lost in the cool breeze and hazy moments of serenity quickly killed by society. I'm falling apart where the road splits discovery's walls. I won't adhere to this disguise. I've found insane ways to follow. Magic is commonplace, and anything can happen, but usually nothing happens at al. It's life for inanimate objects...lazy and crazy demons spring into an overloaded mind. It's just another rehashed opinion. You're just another slave-infested monkey. We're all just rhetoric-stuck monkeys deadened in the heart of man's misconceptions...a chin-splitting catastrophe and a candle aflame...a noble stinking in riches...no name...a freak totally split worlds burning ashes...I spit. It's intelligence feeding off the stupidity of masses...and that's the true definition of politics.

CHAPTER 9

Classical Stomp

A classical stomp or free-floating metaphor stretches the imagination thin. Let's build a bridge to go across into awakening where Christ reins supreme. I'm a spinning slave no more, but this is still a sticky world sometimes. There's sticky sins grabbing at my heels, but they can't keep me down like before. I'm still getting stuck from time to time...under water now. I can't completely feel, and I'm not completely stuck. There's a little freedom though it's not much. Now I'm keeping my head in the clouds and watching slaves from the other side of the glass. On hill tops of sorrow and sad melancholy death breeds life into toy soldiers. With eyes beyond nights brigade the skies open wide swallowing souls. Millions of gods with stone faces leave slaves in sulken fright.

Calm the soul and ease the mind-like spirits...drench in sacred wine...burn incense across the plain because scented smoke kills the pain...cascading water spouts and stifled snows...acres and acres and acres of century's thoughts...no one knows where to go or what to do.

Gaze at the meteor. See where a hyphened ridge in folklore reigns supreme. I have seen another world...a place to hide our bones, a maze to build our homes...a town to plant our dreams and another soul that needs to be redeemed. Now what did you get to see? Who did you get to be? Maybe a mind-controlled, battered click or a misled, brainwashed flea.

All around…out there spirits carry the burden of sophistication and intelligence…overloaded and stupid crazy thoughts and stomach pain. There's got to be a better way…another thought process worth pursuing…maybe rebirth and strange inconsistency. Too much order leads to chaos. Chaos leads to a semblance of a new order. Yet it's all recycled oppression. Self-created gods, we are taught to be and pretend to be. Dead spirits are walking corpses.

Watch the wind trickle down my spine and hear her breath cascade down my vine. Tulip marchers are searching for sunshine…bright and deadly sunshine.

CHAPTER 10

Wealth and Hell Being

Into the abstract, learn the rhetorical stare…study the words: its practitioners preach…nod in agreement…disapprove occasionally…just to mix it up. Constant mental traffic leads to blood clots…the cold shot…the amnesia lot…where memories rot. All things under Christ and His protection and love…dispassionate continuities of grandeur…with hypocrites wearing fancy dress: it's all a grand charade…a mental parade that dulls the side sense of deprecation. Hold your head up and drain your souls' remains: that's what I said…just top it off…contain yourself though. This beautiful imagery…completely nauseous with self-abasement added…getting into the core now. Around the eyes, the beetles hold sway…you see sprinkles of light and no communication…views that slip to the back of the brain where knowledge is contained and left rotting…under another sun.

It's seesaw-seesaw-seesaw battle in the brain…battle in the brain…maybe I'm insane…maybe you're insane. A predominate outpouring if disengaged flesh is haunting your ecstasy further…you must admit your enchantment is calling you on into the Blue Light, the electric night…come on: let's explore…and it's a seesaw-seesaw-seesaw battle in the brain…battle in the brain…a battle for a muscle that will disappear…spirit built on a rock…the rock…my rock:

understand? Crazy and diminutive, we castrate…our view holds sway as the shy leader of the cognitive rationale. There's shifty predawn jaunts into telepathic renewal…through the abstract core, I drift…I drift…I drift deeper into the spiritual realm…where I wish to stay…and never leave.

About the Author

This book is about abstract subject matter. The author uses poetic and philosophical themes to try and explain the unknown. He tries through poetic words to explain that which is unexplainable. His writing style tries to describe that which is lightly touched upon but never fully known.

www.ingramcontent.com/pod-product-compliance
Lightning Source LLC
Chambersburg PA
CBHW050348290526
45785CB00006B/2690